Chorale at the Crossing

Peter Porter

Chorale at the
Crossing

PICADOR

First published 2015 by Picador
an imprint of Pan Macmillan
20 New Wharf Road, London N1 9RR
Associated companies throughout the world
www.panmacmillan.com

ISBN 978-1-5098-0169-5

1 3 5 7 9 8 6 4 2

A CIP catalogue record for this book is available from the British Library.

Printed and bound by CPI Group (UK) Ltd, Croydon, CR0 4YY

Contents

Introduction

The poet Douglas Dunn remembers being on a poetry reading tour with Peter Porter in the West Country in the early 1970s. They were relaxing by having tea in a hotel lounge – or at any rate, Dunn was – as he later realized that there among the chintz and the rexine-covered copies of *The Field* and *Country Life* Porter had also been discreetly at work on a poem. This was probably 'The Castle Hotel, Taunton', from the 1975 volume *Living in a Calm Country*; its loaded closing question, 'But where do the people of England live?' now seeming more pertinent than ever. Poetry was not second nature to Porter: it was the constant forefront of experience. It comes as no surprise that he continued to work for as long as he could after the onset of his final illness. Towards the end he would read drafts aloud so that his wife, Christine, could type poems on to the word processor.

When Don Paterson and I were assembling *The Rest on the Flight: Selected Poems* – the final draft of which appeared only days before the poet's death – Peter was able to give us a new poem to add to the volume: 'After Schiller'. In it the speaker declares, seemingly from beyond the grave:

> *My richness now is nothing but a dearth*
> *Of tricks for the wiping-away of tears.*

There is a slight echo here of Chidiock Tichbourne's Elizabethan lament 'My prime of youth is but a frost of cares' where the cruel negations delivered by imminent execution take a particularly condensed form. A set of associations extends from Tichbourne via Shakespeare to Schiller, Shakespeare's German counterpart. As the bold metrical variations of the second line indicate, this is something more than literariness: as in drama, the lines reveal how they must be spoken, in this case in order to register how enormous sophistication issues from what seems unanswerable plainness. The labyrinthine network of Porter's imagination also presents the possibility that the Shakespearean affirmation 'ripeness is all' is being considered as a conclusion possible in aesthetic terms but far harder to apply to the disorder of actual experience. 'After Schiller', an example of 'late work' if ever there was one, really belongs here, in *Chorale at the Crossing*, a posthumous selection of otherwise uncollected poems, mostly from the period following *Better than God*.

Porter's interests – art, music, literature, history and human affairs in general – are so wide that the work gathered here is, in a sense, instantly familiar; yet these poems also extend the map of his imagination. Porter wrote about death from the very beginning. Haunted by the early death of his mother, he was intimately familiar with mortality and yet unable to comprehend, or sometimes even to admit, this strangest and most imperious of facts. In *Chorale at the Crossing* the world has at some points grown barer, the human position more exposed, as on the lonely shoreline of 'Hermit Crab', as Christine Porter writes in the Afterword. While there are signs of a final move towards a bold plainness among these poems, Porter's large repertoire of tones – and of sheer *material* – remains fully employed. The aphorist, for example, is still mordantly at work when discarding Dante's cosmology:

> *The love which moves the sun and other stars*
> *Is not found here and seems unknown on Mars.*

The long-established Porterian genre of art-biography poems, which would fill a volume in themselves, is also fully operational.

The remarkable 'A Daughter's Life', at once poised and musically mobile, is drawn from a self-portrait by Tintoretto's daughter, Mariella Robusti. It is a rich and beautiful meditation on art, music, faith and the beautiful and brutal city of Venice, from the viewpoint of a woman whose task is self-effacement, and whose self, it seems, is most fully realized in the painting she undertakes:

> *I lick the silver spoon,*
> *draw fever from the moon*
> *and watch the ends of life embrace each other,*
> *meticulously limning*
> *a self to leave behind.*

Formally this could hardly be more remote from Porter's great poem of mourning, 'An Exequy', from the 1978 volume *The Cost of Seriousness*, but there is a comparable contained dignity here. It indicates what range he possessed. The transformation from the roistering satirist of sex, money and the city, in Porter's early career, to this melancholy composure again brings Shakespeare to mind. For Porter was pre-eminently a dramatic poet, for whom Browning remained a presiding presence. Browning's own death in Venice at Ca' Rezzonico is imagined in 'A Toccatina of Galuppi's'. Written in Browningesque rhyming tercets, in lines of seven stresses that flex and scurry by turns, it suggests something of the sheer practicality that has to go into the making of poems as into any art. One of the pleasures of art is that there's a lot of it – and Porter was able to attend to more of it than most.

After his last visit to Australia in 2008, Porter's country of birth seems to figure less in the poems, and there is, for all their richness and reach, a sense of the inevitable shrinking of horizons, leading towards a room he had many times imagined. Thanks to the love and care of Christine, Porter was able to spend his last days at home in their flat, high above a square in Bayswater, where he had lived for over forty years. When I look back on many visits to the flat – which was reached by slogging up what felt like a hundred stairs that Porter cheerfully managed several times a day whilst in his eighties – it seems that elevation conferred a sort of metaphysical advantage, a privileged intensity of seeing, of the kind that Peter sought out in favoured painters such as Pontormo. 'Life is a dream, or very nearly', he wrote in an early poem. Indeed. Readers may count themselves lucky to be invited to enter such an epic and various dreamscape, with such an extraordinary soundtrack, as the poems of Peter Porter.

SEAN O'BRIEN
Newcastle, 17 June 2015

Chorale at the Crossing

First Poem of the Last Book

The creature-comfort sonnets hide themselves
In archives of the brain: set to undo
Both personality and the spermal glue
Of first ambition, destined for high shelves,
They've judged their skills unready, tail-less twelves
Among fourteens, prosodically askew –
They reason tiresomely, and ask, are you
The Blakean worm by night, the one that delves?

Lace me up, Dickensian command!
All my loose versifying I abjure,
Confession's drip, self-pity's one-night stand.
In this new book, no reaching for Last Things,
Not Nature's, God's, or History's armature,
Just kitchen, garden, bedroom splinterings!

After Schiller

Where was I and what then happened to me
When half-light moved beyond eclipse?
Didn't I foresee the end, and you agree
Love is the clumsiest of partnerships?

And would you wish to hear me speak to you
Of irretrievable darkness by the sea;
Of happiness too far off to travel to
And in some narrow space a leafless tree?

The sound of speech, the voice of sense on earth,
In this adjunct seems carpentered of years.
My richness now is nothing but a dearth
Of tricks for the wiping-away of tears.

Moving further, may I find again
The nub of things we shared – the bridal face
Whose hurt if mine was not mine to explain
But made to seem a human commonplace?

With looking upwards hardly in my power
And being forced to seek the stars on earth,
In this exacting planisphere I cower:
I have not moved one footstep from my birth.

Weightless in everlasting space, but true
To the blindly heavy rules of time,
I have become a harbinger for you
Of every weighted station of your climb.

Goodbye to All Cats

For Roger and Patricia

Smart's cat was a smart cat.
I have never had a cat so clever.
But Claudius is a better name than Jeoffrey.

This the Syntax Cat,
it likes its sunlight and its praise
as nicely served up as its dinner.

As our last cat died, its urine on the table
the colour of Prussic Acid, I resolved
to rely on plants for Lifestyle hues.

What a beautiful pussy you are, you are!
You won't mind being banished with Lear
to the remotest most ambivalent star.

The Cat of Simple Statements.
Here. Yes. You. Me. Them.
What? Speak to my Agent.

Both the Country Cat and the City Cat
indulge in normal shudders
when they meet the Vegetarian Cat.

The more terrible dream recurs.
It is about death and is wholly stupid.
No place in it for any sort of cat.

Farewell, my darlings! Godwin, Messalina,
Agrippina, Nero, Claudius and Flora,
Zack and Pip and Mocha. Faded into light.

Gawping at Geckos

Stasis of a Roman Legion,
old forced marches in their legs,
down a wall to the paint's
impersonation of composure.

We match them to our own shade cards;
unchanging yet chameleon,
tepidly green and powdery
like Darwin's bossy fossils.

Somehow more Assyrian than the lizards,
unsententious as the Gate
at Nimrod; scale is the difference,
a model maquette of a lion-hunt.

We nominate this pinkish wall
for a pasquinade of indolence
and watch the geckos superscribe
the here and now hurrying.

From Scribblings on the 'Two Cultures'

The love which moves the sun and other stars
is not found here and seems unknown on Mars.

Random Ageist Verses

Here is the body fearfully beautiful,
The pushy you of just nineteen –
How could you know, in shin or skull,
What's dead already in the sheen?

Immersed in time, we question time
And ask for commentator's rights.
The amoeba has a taste of slime
Among its range of appetites.

It's always too early to die – Oh, yuss!
Says Churchill, dew-lapped TV hound
To The Man on the Clapham Omnibus –
The ice-cap's melting; seek high ground!

The relief of growing old – it's easy
To take long views and shun the short.
Consult the frescoes in Assisi:
Ignore the Kinsey and the Hite report.

Like Auden, I have always felt
The youngest person in the room.
His too too solid flesh might melt
And show him God. I'll need a tomb.

"Senex Scintillans" – we're bright
As glazing on a Peking Duck.
The Elderly insist insight
Is not worth much compared to Luck.

Hers is the most convincing face,
"Col tempo" lightly in her hand –
Age lived-through need show no trace
Of lines time likes to draw in sand.

Who is this young architect
At work of death's blank inventory,
Correcting everything correct?
It is Thomas Hardy, OM, he!

"Gone is all my strength and guile,
Old and powerless am I."
So, Joseph Haydn – all the while
Comes "Laus Deo" in reply.

The greyness of the sky is streaked
Along its width with shades of red;
The pity of the world has leaked
But who are these whose hands have bled?

A Toccatina of Galuppi's

O Galuppi, Baldassare, gone for good all Browning's praise,
Those commiserating sevenths, Music Theory's bad-hair days –
Lost are rhythm, assonances, apt conjunction, gnomic phrase.

Hear the keyboard clatter coldly, cautious CDs sitting pretty,
Think the sunlight on Giudecca, haze above the golden city.
Wordless, Goethe, Corvo, Powell! Since the Futurists, who's witty?

Il Buranello yields to Nono, and the kissing's sternly stopped.
The seven maids who for the Walrus and the Carpenter once mopped
Have swept away by now the tearful sand on which the Frari's propped.

Bewildering, your notes cascading through a handful of octaves,
The watertable at Marghera, falling, may expose the graves
And moonlight dousing the piazzas silver the advancing waves.

Past the Zattere, mud-churning, steepled Cruise Ships plumply dock.
The metronome, a silent convert, is attrition's ticking clock
And in San Bastian an expert marks down Veronese's stock.

San Zaccaria's great Bellini ponders *Parsifal* on tape
While Colleoni bumbles fiercely where Stravinsky lay in state.
Ateneo and Accademia authorise Europa's Rape.

What hangs in minor keys and major lingers in the mind like lead.
"Those suspensions, those solutions – must we die?" and then we're dead.
In the Ca' Rezzonico, one Robert Browning climbs to bed.

A Fierce Flower

For Margaret Gregory

For a female observer, a wished-for leader,
Daringly hockey-stick, a commander
Of the *Feminist Fusiliers*;
Stuck in a vase, but able to toss a grenade,
Perfume or petals; might be Dracula's bride.

For a male observer, the flowering of a rival,
Almost erect in the dormitory, could reveal
How to do it, *Sex Without Tears*;
But undeniably a handsome predator,
Low-slung, draping his cloak like a matador.

Now change to Neuter Gender: "Linnean Comrades,
We must fight Humanity on the barricades,
forget our *Watering-Can Tears*;
We have nothing to lose but our clay-bound hearths,
The air is ours and the beauty and the immaculate deaths."

Dorothea Tanning: Eine Kleine Nachtmusik in Tate Modern

When you have lost whatever there is to lose
You will come to the House of Tatterdemalion Proofs
Where reality is always adjacent to itself
And words are at war with their subjunctives –
Alas, you recognize the mildewed Classics,
Blake's Sunflower stranded, Cherubino's hair on fire,
A pair of gloves for clapping the great aria.

How many of these doors have the partygoers knocked at?
Is 210 ajar, waiting to receive someone
Or is it the cupboard where the cleaners keep their dreams?
The carpet on the corridor is on Red Alert.
An official of the Surreal Inspectorate
Is interrogating guests downstairs: *do you now*
Or have you ever belonged to the Accumulative Party?

Life enlarges any neat Divertimento,
So things terrible and beautiful are reborn
Of their own volition; existence may become
A shabby house in a lost Chicago street,
But you cannot dream it otherwise – the lines
Are drawn and the bombardment starts:
Do not wake us yet, our rage must run.

Breakfast at Tiffany's

He walks lopsided but beseechingly correct,
a really good dog, and Martha and I are pleased
we can talk of the way we enjoy being one old
and one young (or is it Millie I'm with this time?) –
thus we're approximated up to the Big House
they've just stripped the ivy from. Off and through a smell
knowing the sheep are now too near the fence,
he'll come back, perhaps from behind the logs
stacked bright and scored with sap; this is the morning
of the world for young and old, still swan-sustaining.

I can't ask her, my sixteen-year-old granddaughter,
how to break my fast on a text so nifty
it's the Unconscious polishing its nails,
the short lines right, the working metaphors
so everyday they're sold at Matalan.
This is Theory though it looks like Verse.
Maybe it's truly emulation, like the day
I joined the toughest gang at school – alas,
in times of fame the 'In House' style is light,
from Bran Flakes to the beach gazetted 'Dogs R Us'.

Another "Fat Boy Special", Bitte.
There's A War On Herr Reger.

I eat for all those fighting at the Front,
Exactly as death eats – he gets plump –
I get to add an "a" or "b" or "bis"
To yet another opus number –
I am the patriot of dumplings.

A "fat-boy special" in the Speisewagen –
Bits from pigs and cows and that Bavarian
Asparagus which whitens on the dead;
There needn't be dark beer,
A wine from France is not apostasy.

"Hier im ird'schen Jammerthal" –
What's there to do but eat our sorrow?
The Magic Bullets are all fired,
The Waldhorn silent in the forest.

A Chip Off the Old Blog

John Knox
is in his box
and his box
is in its hole.

Time locks
the doors of clocks,
a paradox
of Mind and Soul.

The Shuttle docks,
and in detox
Prometheus rocks
in fire he stole.

Lines for an English Heine

I

Our monosyllables are fraught
With all the things we cannot say,
And feeling now is drawn to thought
While thought is threadbare with delay.

The street of houses built secure
Has one side only – opposite
The railway walls raised to immure
The sky are secretly moonlit.

Germanic hopes by tongue-tied lake
In simple language trail the heart,
But English words cannot awake
From secrecy a speaking art.

II

The land is out at sea; we mean
The dead are breaking on the land,
Their lives once like the waves between
The flooding and the drying sand.

On beaches soft philosophers
Learn hardness as their minds entail
Some danger where no movement stirs
An empty shell or drifting sail.

Or were they seeking continents
Drowned years ago whose merchants thought,
As veterans of immanence,
That cargoes would come safe to port?

III

I stand here now where once she stood,
Two girls in tow, our daughters who,
So well-behaved, so tamed to good,
Each one hand at a time withdrew.

My sight should conjure from a space
The person in this bald graveyard;
I touch but cannot see her face,
The same stern angels standing guard

Of whom she scarcely felt aware
Being so close to where they rule.
One is the number of despair
And aggregate of ridicule.

IV

A self-indulgent dreamer –
Or so his fellows thought
Whose visions of completeness
Are what is sold and bought.

Yet he too bought and traded
In civil wish and hope,
His black world reinvaded
By blatant heliotrope.

Thus, in his dreamscape pictured,
The sun, that spectrum'd yell,
Could stream through death's tight fingers
And light the plains of hell.

Letter to John Kinsella

Theology's Hell is spoiled by rhyme –
Let's be spontaneous this time,
Help the Devil up off his back,
Make him the Joker of the Pack
And set that donor on to pay
Evil's pension and delay
The hideous Christian triumph – Sword
Making Word rhyme with Accord.

This toothy Satan has two tits
(Not breasts but iron artefacts)
Whose eye-ball nipples blink at sin
And all the lovely worms within
While God and his pale Myrmidons
Drill Virgins in their Uniforms,
The shock troops of the Interface
Of pissing's and of shitting's place.

What did Despair do when a Christ
Declared no creature was despised,
That He and Dad had love for all
And no-one was outside the Wall?
It smiled and waited till Mankind,
Becoming so much more refined,
Elected Emptiness the Devil
Screened off in some white Hospital.

Back once when Señor Bermejo
Put armoured Righteousness on show
The loyal Public played its part –
The Lord was harsh but Sin was Art:
Victorious Virtue shone on steel,
Piety paid and so might kneel
As witness, but the People knew
That Satan's tail, cut off, regrew.

Every picture tells a story,
Each healing Shrine will be *fuori*
And I can't scathe this painting merely
As Superstition very nearly –
A moral then – if Wars of Style
Are all that Poets find worthwhile
And Inspiration's out of reach,
Stop them writing, let them teach!

A Daughter's Life

from a self-portrait, circa 1590, by Marietta Robusti,
daughter of Jacopo Tintoretto

The distance
from God the Father
to the Father god
is charted in the part-book in my hand —
what we play or sing
is a bequeathing,
manna picked up on Malamocco's sand
as merchants gather
their celestial food.

The daughter
of a great painter
who painted the Great
should be ever dutiful and strict.
"Daddy. I hardly knew
you, my lifetime through."
An artist's task is properly to depict
Christ the Inventor
in Man the Ape.

San Rocco's
paint is music
and its music, paint —
I learned to be at all times smartly dressed.

The ladder of the octave,
its foot set in the grave,
fills with the angels Jacob saw and blessed,
esoteric, ludic,
and beside the point.

By repute
how publicly serene
our Serenissima,
its sun-swept towers, its galleys and its gaols!
This garment's golden thread
runs in my head
while shipwrights hammer home their iron nails
and crane by crane
set death on the water.

And I know
the end of my beginning
is the beginning of my end;
one day a daughter will become a mother.
I lick the silver spoon,
draw fever from the moon
and watch the ends of life embrace each other,
meticulously limning
a self to step behind.

A Swinburne Sugar Rush

On just one bottle of Pale Ale a new
certificated ecstasy is born.
The ladder could start anywhere, and being
slightly sick and considerably mad
I need no drug to flush the confusion out.
Better poets than I use native skills,
the virtual vernacular, to astound
a once religious land (*viz.* Tennyson),
but in my gonged hendecasyllables
I make words choric atoms and not steps
for Greek Philosophers. On star-sanded edges
of imagination everything
is dancing in a formal hecatomb.
I feel the sugar rising in my cheeks;
Madam, a dragée is deathly sweet.

Du Holde Kunst

You have saved me
from the permanent irrelevance of words,
from poems begging in my ears,
from unread novels scowling on the shelves
and things God says, talking in his sleep.

Ich danke dir
I say to the genius in my ear,
where did I leave my keys?

The world will always be Boulez,
Adam thought, after twenty-four hours
of listening to the brook –

trees to be pleached,
cuttings to be spliced,
animal droppings hunkered in.
I can invent an art
free of everything but mathematics,
he told the insects,
a special sort of noise for human brains.

Australian Literary Graffiti

If you should propose
to Peter Rose,
'Give up the opera, mate!',
he'd simply not cooperate.

'We're not fighting flab,'
states Chris Wallace-Crabbe,
as he steps out on court:
'This is Poets for Sport.'

'Modernism absorbs
the past,' claims John Forbes.
'There's much of *East Lynne*
in Jeremy Prynne.'

'It doesn't hurt to kneel,'
explains Peter Steele.
'Your verse needn't plod
because there's a God.'

David Malouf
once was aloof
but since leaving Tuscany
he's become almost buskiny.

Ron Simpson
is like Gulley Jimson,
an unpainted wall
holds him in thrall.

Expressions of pain
are heard in Balmain:
'To your desk, Tranter!'
cries Lynn, his Infanta.

Robert Gray
spends part of each day
staring at the ceiling
hearing the 'True Voice of Feeling'.

Peter Carey
avoids Port Fairy,
he prefers the harsh
tracts of Bacchus Marsh.

Havelock Ellis
said, 'Listen, Fellers,
sex can derail yer
even in Australia.'

Three for Les

From Taree to Surrey
the world knows Les Murray.
His tone is 'Consult you all',
not Multicultural.

The Poets of Mildura
could hardly be purer,
they all honour Les
and do what he says.

In his Canberra coterie
each one's a Notary
and every subpoena is
sworn to his genius.

The Poet Porter's Old Age Hope

To ride the surf
at Soixante-neuf
and stay at the crease
at Soixante-dix.

In the event he
doesn't reach seventy,
he's determined to shine
at Sixty-nine.

The Long March of Cornelius Cardew

The hardest road, the hardiest foot on stone,
the unrolled bandage latticed with dried blood –
Great Truth alone can justify 4/4.
We keep the palimpsestic scores in racks,
in hives of apian tyranny, the wax so soft
and yet so diligent, a thousand, more two thousand
years of pain notated by control,
the delta'd varicose of a society
the which I said I loathed until
I heard Stockhausen damn it with
his apotheosis of Unhistory.
I knew at once his will was deathlier
than anything the Classics ever did,
the bead-games, tombs and truant nightingales.
If there were a Yangtze so immense
it dwarfed its river self, I know I'd hear
the left-right feet make music round
all temples, sepultures, stockyards, bus-stops,
a unison chromatically complete,
a march as fixed as hope, as long as sky.

I don't regret my absolutist scores,
at least they're beautiful to look at;
I am the son of a Ceramicist.
Someone saw Heaven once and it resembled
a circuit-board beyond Aldebaran,
panelled and personified, sure proof

that everything which is intelligent
waits its decay to only loveliness.
But still the march goes on. As always, the river
is beside us, its syncopated waves
a proper counterpoint to common time.
Already we have passed the brazen gate
of Capitalism, obliging life to share
its dividends with us – if epic poetry
gives way to peasant tunes, the reason is
it can't be sung downline; the city needs
to know the desert's proud intent,
that millions in their locust coats shall stand
beneath the walls of Old Metonymy,
and just one voice to magistrate the air.

The Novelist's Visitors

The first was like a man in a novel:
he said bastard rich novelists
owed a duty to people like him
who had been shat on all their lives –
to take them in and care for them – he'd slept
in a park for five nights and had no money
and nowhere to go. He was coming round now
to stay – he'd be with him in a minute or two.
The novelist used to answer such importunates
by pulling rank, usually speaking of a family loss,
an unexpected death, a niece, a cat, even
once his wife. Somehow this time he couldn't say
a word. He put the phone down and locked the door
and waited. He sat up most of the night
but nobody came. He read later of a man
under a train at Uxbridge – read and wondered.
How was it that it was the messenger who died?

The second visitor was not his visitor
but someone he was visiting. Not really visiting
though he was there in bed with her. He was learning
how hard it is to get away, knowing he didn't
want to be where he was, but thinking
his impotence was old age, not regret or guilt –
if she were keen there were so many ways she could
assist him. But pillow-talk stayed with the novel
and she couldn't grasp that proper grammar

is no impediment to experiment
and its insistences. If both she and he were hardly there
another presence must be in the bed, another
struggling ghost for whom the daylight world
was an alibi of night. But who was this?
He would not court his dreams – too quixotic,
irresponsible, sharply known and feared.
Such loving scorn must lead to someone's death.

A third and proving time he knew his visitor
the winged and helmeted soul-collector and so spoke
of how he'd waited all his life for this
and written him in every book, and spoken of him
on a hundred platforms – ask his readers.
Yet was he sure? Authenticity might have
so many aliases. From Sophocles till now words
had fed on writers' doubts: the questions had no answer
or posed as silly riddles. That's why books were written
and stories gathered in the mind like pollen on bees' legs:
the stranger at the crossroads might be your sire
or the spectre in the plague cart. The doubt was still
that any could discern the form of Hermes,
a murderer on a boat or an auxiliary postman:
there'd be a novel in this, he told himself,
though he doubted, like Dickens, he'd ever know
which street tonight his death was walking down.

It's the Gravity, Stupid

Whatever else could make the heart so heavy,
The muscles round the bowels a constant strain,
The truth that Upside owes Downside a levy
And Sisyphean blood must reach the brain?

It needn't be so, says the Man in Space,
His airborne screwdriver strapped to his wrist;
A weightless dance has a colloidal grace,
In Physics the whole Universe seems pissed.

A huge Iambics shapes Morality —
It states there's no alternative until
Mathematics shall abandon Middle C
And fresh meat be anterior to the kill.

They've stitched up Newton, these who'll also die:
Disinterested as ever, I start "I . . .

Look-Alikes

I happened on a vista – it was in Antwerp
and I couldn't believe my eyes (I don't want
to believe any of my senses) but it was there –
Fouquet's tennis-ball-breasted pale Madonna
and her scarlet ball-boy angels – (I knew
Agnès Sorel never met Picasso) –
I had painted that picture often in my mind
when I was nineteen. How did it get there?
I hadn't thought of it for years – I'd have
never given it the right to worry me again.
Who'd want to revisit his tormented youth?

Later I saw some photographs of flayed
and tortured animals, a vivisection montage
down High Street Kensington and straightway
made the wrong connection. I wanted to eat
a hamburger and relish shades
of red and gold in Marsyas's skinning.
How serviceable to throw the switch on living,
promote a new ascendancy, pure
intentionalism, the chance to share
with teeth and eyes a straight depravity.

A Versatile Myth

The remarkable disaster sings and pleases;
it was someone's fault and the widening world
had too many tomorrows to endure –
so they invented Orpheus and his one mistake,
looking back at love for fear he wouldn't
recognize it – music had the stamp of loss
from the beginning, a search for melody.

Now for the adaptations: out of that garden
the Wrong of Wrongs, a Hebrew or a Greek
belabouring, "quo abiit dilectus tuus",
booked into Heaven and reluctant; the keeper
of infinitude who sang to die.

A Perfect Suicide

And here I will sacrifice all rhyme,
that is, I will avoid any of the beautiful
consequences which may intrude on patterns
infinitely more inter-calculable – I shall
be in a world of egregious simplicity,
protected by a cold dependency.

Yet I bungled my own death,
kept alive for days trying to analyse
for friends and fellow-architects
why melancholy has a concave shape
and whether heaven, ordered to design
a ceiling, would stand in its own light.

Seeing is beneath believing, which is why
air is stonier than its vista – as on my portrait
the set-squares and the compasses make Signs
of the Cross more Christian than the Cross
upon my breast and sleeve. The Pyramids
were told that weight was Incarnation.

Socrates died of a morphic sort of rictus,
Seneca in a steamy froth of blood,
I with a muddle of indignity and plans.
To kill oneself as perfectly as a line
will reach a tributary line
is masonry continuing in one stay.

On the Best Battlefields No Dead Bodies

Death is unfit for anything but writing about.
On *The Antiques Roadshow* it adopts the posture
of an Eighteenth Century culverin
which should be insured for Fifteen Hundred Pounds
and still we know how much it costs to cast
a trainee pilot in a jet into the Irish Sea.
It is happily content to be
'the trigger of the Literary Man's biggest gun',
hating, as it does, both noise and smells,
and bikes to work masked as a Tokyo commuter.
Itself its favourite word, it is as politic
as Faith and lets statistics arabesque
those glaciers that melt and birds which leave their eggs;
it is in perfect taste even for an Age
which has no taste –

                touch it as you touch yourself
in commentary or horror – there's nothing there.
Superior to rhyme, it lives in poems
'that will never die'.

              It says, a lover of quotation,
its glory is it had such friends
and a refrigerated Heaven to retire to.
And now the Poet tells what might be true –
she was made a legatee of battlefields,

This title is derived from Veronica Forrest-Thomson's 'Lemon and Rosemary'.

of every pibroch and retreat across the years
and affirms that no-one dies,
no word or ward is lost –
instead, and scattered round,
all that she sees is offered to the gods,
the hasty permanence of sanity.

Poem Shorter Than its Epigraph

"Du wollest dem Feinde nicht geben
die Seele deiner Turteltauben." *

Beaks above,
claws beneath,
teeth below —
the soul invents
its enemies.

* J. S. Bach, Cantata No. 71.

The Singverein of Abstinence

I'm writing this poem hoping to placate
One of my more forensic critics who
Considers the titles of my poems ridiculous.

Though perhaps not more so than their contents.
If so, how, in vernacular terms, should I,
Someone educated in the reticence

Of Middle-Class respectability, record
My lifelong fear of conquistadorial
Masculinity, my quaking at the password

Opening up Avernus's vaginal gardens –
'Knock and be admitted' – but I am not
That famous black and darting Crow which pecks

Its way through every female passage. Not
To be investingly erect suggests
A predetermined clerk-like way with words,

And so I choose this German noun, a trope
Derived from music, that to be discreet,
Lofted from loss to magnanimity

And following in how-so-many parts,
Affected to arouse through childhood vistas
A diapason round the burning pit.

Some Men in Starbucks

They hope their daughters are still fond of them
And recognize their best side, as their wives didn't
Viz, those other days they sat in Coffee Bars
And, contrite, found themselves still chidden.

Both wives and mistresses, companioned now
By a second Age of sickly Discontent,
Love their apprentice daughters, but complain
That what's inherited need pay no rent.

The men will have the worst of it: the taste
Of coffee is more bitter than the loss
Of ignorance, more draining than regret.
Will she just wave or will she move across?

Your Considerate Stone

The writer's, not the martyr's task, to be
a dolmen studied for its evidence
of what has passed this way. You search the web
for far-back genitors, bearded builders,
maiden aunts, to find within yourself
the Easter Island statues of your sort,
blind presences where time itself was stalled,
determining the way that shadows lie.

Approximate a *Grabmal*, not as plain
as headstones you have never bothered with
where, peregrine, your family is at rest
except that little civic cemetery
bathed in elm-light, where the London train
may seem to stop and the Parish Church's
Visitors' Book holds entries for Anubis –
what there was written, you have had to hear.

The world your stone, the world as stone,
a draining of their energy from watchers
of persistence. A person may step down
from a dream and yet not come to you –
you must come to her. And if your heart's
a hardened gallstone, it might claim
consideration of its species' quality,
the hardest of hard things inherited.

The Downside

To wonder about the Afterlife
is natural up to Keats's age
but is just an avenue of clocks
tracing unmeasured days
when you might die at any moment.
Don't lament what you have written,
remember the stack of untouched paper
which will excuse you. At school
you could magic words off any page –
gone, they were the best words in the world.

And the small exemplary lives
which helped to build the great cathedrals
are with us still. Here is the incinerator
your Father burned his leaves in:
there is the great book of the *Inferno*
where hate has a part for everyone –
perhaps you had a hand in it? – on the other side,
as people say. Once you have a calling
you know you will be called for.

Silkworms Work and Love Till Death

He kept a list of poems there were to write,
A personal list, imperative and sour –
Beyond his windows all was digital,
The nominative unpleasantness of thought
Recurred, he reasoned, every day in speech.
He feared the public knew the thing he was,
And one of those who would not be alone.

In blood one day he framed a strategy,
The curt unpitied sadness of a sage
He read about at some South China Court
Who slated certainty and cut up sights
To keep them small – Of course you must still write,
The Master wrote, but little that you mean:
Your paper should not die to prove your words.

Ex Abrupto

Here was I compulsively
shouldering the jaws of birth,
construing the dip into Avernus,
facing the Gates of Paradise,
yet losing count of time, a son
too old to be a prodigal.

The Castaway is Washed Ashore

She was the ship I sailed in, or
      We twinned as just one ship,
A Mother and a Son, assured
      Of one another's grip:
We guessed it wouldn't be for life,
A boy becalmed, a seasoned wife.

Whatever, there would come the storm,
      The light propitious fade;
Suburban living was the norm,
      A slovenly parade.
Which one would fall, which doomed to drown,
If climbing up were settling down?

The storm would blow us separately –
      For her, poor doctoring,
Stifled in her own blood's sea,
      I, at her skirts to cling.
Then Education's sad voice hit
My ears and I joined mine to it.

Out on the selfish ocean tossed,
      The storm now just a squall,
Apocalypse the only Cross
      And that equivocal:
My *placement* was below the salt,
A setting? Or a Primal Fault?

A second ship: this was another
          Woman marked to die.
No strong resemblance to my Mother,
          But, like her, serving my
Absurd disintegration, took
The black she needed from a book.

Mixed metaphors sail on apace,
          The ship goes down, and then
A second time the splintered face,
          A Castaway again –
A pair of ragged claws might row
Me safely from the undertow.

Quotation like a flag unfurled
          In cruel convenience,
Showed my position in the world,
          The past my present tense.
As mushrooms rose the childish faces,
A succulence of desert places.

As if in time's conjunctions, I
          Flew past the sugared peaks
Of Greenland – portholes bled the sky
          For Frequent Flyer geeks –
Life had to make its proffered run
Between extinction and the sun.

Such was the beach I scrambled up,
　　　Like Crusoe seeming saved,
The storm still simmered in its cup
　　　Which through my dreams had raved.
The mind, that navigating hand,
Now sought to drown me on the land.

An Absolutist Chorale

Our God is here, a practical recruitment,
The millions he has killed he cannot see.
He is the Sorry One, the swarm precipitant,
And his an executioner's privacy.

To be alone is every person's gift,
Though crying in the night is a reminder
That Happy Valleys are Repression's Rift.
Confession looks best in a sombre binder.

And these, the very neatest hymns, are made
Not for the Faithful or the purloined critics
But just to show that rebels can't evade
The hiccups, plump Aristotelian Ethics.

The world should get much better – yes, it should.
It tries, it surely does. What interposes
We're never sure of. Facing what is good
We smell the blood: we cannot smell the roses.

Salon of Lost Masterpieces

To open the invitation is to fear infarction
at the breakfast table – oh, if you could get there,
Rush Hour traffic being what it is, and tickets
difficult to come by. And bringing to mind
the last occasion your dilatoriness so shamed you –
that miraculous Exhibition, impossible to repeat,
"Prodigies of Post-Intentionalism",
the ultimate extravagance of European Art:
what Cimabue turned his back on, what Duccio
let Lippo di Memmo execute instead, the medals
Pisanello felt he hadn't quite the skill for, two Pieros
neglecting frescoes in the name of health and sanctity,
Caspar David dying before he set his easel up
at the confluence of the Neckar and the Rhine, Turner's
conspectus of the masculine pudenda, the bluest
Swimming Pool Hockney found untenanted –
perhaps all this should be left for later – if what was lost
has now been found, our human satisfaction might
accept its fearful heritage of richness
and let the worthless world shine for itself.

For Christine

I have caught a late boat and see you
      against the rail: you are both me
      and the sea – you are (for this is a dream)
      looking for me as I am for you,
      but we have responsibilities
      towards the sea and when we touch
      waves applaud against the side.

It makes more sense to think of us
      happy and perturbed in Italy –
      your insisting only a Greek could sculpt
      such limbs beneath the marble robe
      and my subtraction of the glory
      by some Roman dating. Our love is based
      on the different ways we cross a road.

And then there are the words we suck
      out of each other and the space between,
      the interface on which a phrase
      is also history, the heritage we own
      of human harm, the mothers and sons,
      the fathers and daughters, broken hearts
      to share among the broken-hearted.

Like all true love it turns to air
      when aired by cool analysis:
      I weep by the waters of

recorded art; you adopt the missionary's
best position, listening and likening –
our selfish cats convey between
us the essential messages.

Being educated enough to know
about correlatives, objective ones
and otherwise, we comprehend
the daily life we share – how just
that what the boys of Naples tried
to steal were books on Freud and Mozart,
in with the cardigans and tissues.

I raise my pen as if it were a glass
and write a toast to you: drink me,
as life asked Alice to, I am
the stuff that's meant for you, and you
the food my eyes have commandeered –
it's late, but Autumn in the Square
defines how Summer will return.

What are all the names for love –
the cautious and the cautionary,
the exhilarating and the murderous,
the afternoon, alarmed and weary,
the long way back over difficult ground,
the prospect from the tower of sleep,
the lock-up soundly, we've come home?

A Chorale at the Crossing

Ihr Gatten, die ihr liebend euch in Armen liegt,
ihr seid die Brücke, überm Abgrund ausgespannt,
auf der die Toten wiederum ins Leben gehn!
Geheiliget sei eurer Liebe Werk!

Hugo von Hofmannsthal

But that one who is the very always one
May still be a surprise – if she's whom
That time you betrayed and this time rebuked,
Who, while you were thinking of another,
Startled you by not wanting to be with you
Though you'd excused all othernesses
By resolving to make her the true centre
Of existence; accepting that this was
Accounting, a way of excusing betrayal
By ordering responsibility –
Then, and no surprise after all
It should be so, the uncontrollable dream
Showed not her but you; not life but death.

This message be the message of the bridge the dead
Walk over; they are sparkling in their chances
However undeserving; they have been dressed
In time's immeasurability;

One life could never be enough; their tunes
Are faces, their words perfectly understandable
Yet have no meaning. This side of the bridge
There is a toll – it's like the seventy stairs
You have been up and down a million times;
It is paid in lifetime familiarity.
Now they are seen to be carrying, everyone
The same burden, the command to love,
Where some object might exist as proof
Or all the stars collate the obligation.

Hermit Crab

I have no new shell to retreat to
Having scanned the beach (it has never
Seemed so wide and such a tympanum
For the thundering ocean) and watched the gulls
Hanging their banners of transformation
Across the sky, I used to believe
That this shell I soon must leave
Was the only shell I have ever lived in,
Perhaps I was remembering the glorious nacre
Of the home I was introduced to
When first I looked about me
And which protected me in ways
I did not recognize. Sometimes
I recall other shells as a long symposium
Stretching in a clockless aura —

But always and ever shells upon the beach.

How cold the beach and lonely,
The last domain of light's remembering.
Without a home, one made of current comforts
And loving faces, forgetting
Becomes impossible, and yet the silence
Of the beach, the missing sun
And time-tied stars show
Everything's forgotten and I can forget.

Afterword

A NOTE ON 'HERMIT CRAB'

'Hermit Crab', written in the last year of Peter's life, is for me both a daunting and very special poem. I found it on my computer some months after he died; it was dated 23 February 2010, just six weeks before he passed away. As his body became weaker, I would type poems for him. I recall his presence working through me, slowly and carefully guiding my hands as I worked.

This poem is, for me, a powerful hymn to death and the letting-go of life. Peter uses the image of the hermit crab to convey his lifelong experience of protecting the most vulnerable, delicate and fragile parts of himself. But here he also finds himself in another moment of transition from one state of being to another; he fears there are no more shells, no further protection for vulnerable, exposed flesh – or, indeed, for the sometimes fragmentary and defenceless mind.

The hermit crab is born without a shell of its own, and has to borrow its protection from other creatures – a temporary home. It's a simple metaphor, saying that perhaps – as vulnerable human creatures, with an insecure sense of self – we take on the carapace of those we see as better able to survive. But when we outgrow the shell's usefulness, we are once again vulnerable and exposed, once again forced to seek another form of psychic protection.

But the speaker of this poem seems to be saying that in those times of transition, instead of dissolving or fragmenting (and perhaps through the very creation of this poem) he finds that while he may not have the shell to protect him, he has instead the nacre – the mother-of-pearl inner lining of a shell or 'eggshell'. This is the aura of the mother, at the very beginning of life. It is her mind and being that will nurture this new and fragile self.

Peter was born in Brisbane, Australia on 16 February 1929, the only child of Marion and William, or at least the only live birth for this couple. Marion, according to Peter, had five miscarriages, and Peter would describe himself as 'the only one to get through'. Peter's mother died when he was nine years old. He came home from school one day to be told that his mother was in hospital. She had, in effect, disappeared. The morning had been quite ordinary.

When he thought back, Peter could not quite recall the last time he actually saw his mother. He was never taken to the hospital to see her; all he seemed to remember was being told she had died. This will have been a catastrophic disappearance for a nine-year-old child. I sense something of that early catastrophe within this poem, written some seventy years after the event.

As the poet gathers together something from this early experience, then perhaps 'a thundering ocean' resembles the foetal sense of the mother's heartbeat and inner body at the moment of realizing its own existence. It is also something outside of oneself, a palpable other, a sense of our own smallness and terrifying aloneness and separateness. That primordial sense of otherness in such small creatures is indeed terrifying, and perhaps hardly forms anything like a bearable thought or a shaped experience for such a small being, unaware that it is as yet separate from anything.

What the old dying poet seems to know is that letting go of life evokes such things that might have haunted their own sense of being from life's very foundation. The moment when the body goes cold and still is the moment when an ocean again inhabits the mind. Once again, the 'other' makes itself palpably felt; but by now we know the 'other' may mean one's own extinction.

Peter's sense of displacement, of not quite belonging to the world, was a very important part of him; he always felt himself to be something like an 'air plant', a being without roots. In the middle section of 'Hermit Crab' there seems to be a kind of reconciliation with his lost mother, a deep awareness that it was *she* who provided the nacre, the skin, the breathable atmosphere within which he was able to assemble himself and grow. For me, it was relief to realize that he could finally acknowledged his gratitude to her. The experience of gratitude in its self recognizes the gift the sacrifice the mother makes for her child, allowing him a space in her mind.

When a parent dies while the child is young, both the sense of abandonment and the reflexive self-blaming are acute and overwhelming. As a species, the first instinctive assumption we make upon being abandoned by such an important, life-giving presence is that it was, or is, *our fault*. This is much more so in small children, as the thought is less a formed thought than an overwhelming sense – a sense that we have been too demanding, too greedy, or simply too much for the parent to have managed.

With all that in mind, I find the last stanza of 'Hermit Crab' very poignant. Here the poet returns to the future, where feeling and thought become somewhat bleak: 'how cold and lonely' the beach is. Peter struggled with the idea of a home, a place were he was at least partly known – but nonetheless the 'current comforts and loving faces' helped to ease him into a place where 'forgetting becomes possible', and made letting go, leaving behind the life he loved, just slightly more bearable.

CHRISTINE PORTER
July 2015